This
Note Book
belongs
To

Thank You

We hope you enjoyed

As a small family company, your feedback is very important to us.

Please let us know how you like our notebook at:

mirelaheljbook@yahoo.com